THE DEPUTATION TRAIL
MINISTRY
OR
A MEANS TO AN END?

Missionary & Pastor Jeremy Markle

WALKING IN THE WORD MINISTRIES

Missionary/Pastor Jeremy Markle
www.walkinginthewordministries.net

*Missions: The Deputation Trail
Ministry or a Means to an End?*
by Missionary/Pastor Jeremy Markle

All rights reserved solely by the author.
No part of this book may be reproduced, stored in a retrieval system, or transmitted in any form or by any means – electronic, mechanical, photocopy, recording, or otherwise – without written permission of the author.

Unless otherwise noted, all Scripture quotations are from the King James Version.

Copyright © 2015 by Pastor Jeremy Markle.

Edited by PEP Writing Services
pepwritingservices.com

Published by Walking in the WORD Ministries
www.walkinginthewordministries.net

Printed in the United States of America

ISBN 978-0692415184

I wish to lovingly dedicate this book
to my wife, Laura,
who has faithfully joined me
in every aspect of my life and ministry.

Special Thank You

To PEP Writing Services
for editing services
and to Pastor Scott Markle
for help with the cover design.

CONTENTS

FROM MY HEART TO YOUR HANDS	1
DEPUTATION PHILOSOPHY	3
Ministry or Misery	5
Be a Servant and Dont Get Used to Being Served	11
Initiative or Impatience	15
Patience or Complacency	17
Pastoral Relationships and Respect	19
Supernatural Provision or a Sales Pitch	23
Beggars Cant Be Choosers, or Can They?	27
From a Glass House to a Glass Suitcase	35
Faithfulness or Failure	43
Preaching:Performance or Proclamation	45
Time Spent or Time Invested	51
DEPUTATION PRACTICE	55
Helpful Tips	57
SUPPLEMENTARY EXAMPLES	81

FROM MY HEART TO YOUR HANDS

Dear friend, each missionary's deputation experience can be as diverse as the country, culture, and language to which God is guiding him or her to minister. The purpose of this booklet is not to be the final answer to deputation's questions nor to provide the secrets to a fast and easy deputation ministry. Rather, it is intended to help the ministry process by presenting biblically based philosophies and practical tips to guide you through a God-honoring, church-expanding, and believer-edifying prefield ministry.

As I seek to be helpful by documenting a few practical principles for deputation ministry, I am very aware that I am not an expert on the subject. There are individuals who could easily expand on my work and provide a more detailed resource. However, I pray that what I learned during my six months of part-time deputation (which began less than one year after 9/11), two years of full-time travel before language-school training, and six months of travel before leaving for the field with over 100 percent of our budgeted support can be of some help to those who follow. These lessons were not learned in the isolation of my own personal wisdom but through a mixture of personal study and experience, assisted by the counsel and insight of others whom God directed into my life before, during, and after my deputation ministry. There is no doubt that any "success" I saw on deputation was not based on special manmade formulas but on God's graciousness. My deputation trail began with a direct answer to prayer and ended when God provided my last meeting and fulfilled my budget requirements. Therefore, I praise God for His goodness in the lessons I have learned and also for those I have been able to spiritually encourage during this time of ministry travel.

DEPUTATION PHILOSOPHY

A proper philosophy of life and ministry is just as important as sound roots are to a tree. As the roots of a solid tree must be grounded in good soil so that the tree can receive regular nourishment and maintain its stability, so the roots of a proper life and ministry philosophy must be grounded in God's Word in order to provide the needed spiritual nourishment and stability that are required for a life of Christian service.

Psalm 1:1–3 says: *"Blessed is the man that walketh not in the counsel of the ungodly, nor standeth in the way of sinners, nor sitteth in the seat of the scornful. But his delight is in the law of the LORD; and in his law doth he meditate day and night. And he shall be like a tree planted by the rivers of water, that bringeth forth his fruit in his season; his leaf also shall not wither; and whatsoever he doeth shall prosper."*

It is very important that God's servants constantly evaluate not only what they are doing but also the biblical philosophy behind their actions. These servants of God must ensure that they are truly living in God's will, accomplishing it God's way, and doing it for God's glory. They must humbly recognize that I Corinthians 1:27–31 apply to their life and ministry: *"But God hath chosen the foolish things of the world to confound the wise; and God hath chosen the weak things of the world to confound the things which are mighty; And base things of the world, and things which are despised, hath God chosen, yea, and things which are not, to bring to nought things that are: That no flesh should glory in his presence. But of him are ye in Christ Jesus, who of God is made unto us wisdom, and righteousness, and sanctification, and redemption: That, according as it is written, He that glorieth, let him glory in the Lord"* (1 Corinthians 1:27–31).

In the discussion of a missionary's deputation philosophy, John the Baptist's words in John 3:30, *"He must increase, but I must decrease,"* must be exemplified.

The Apostle Paul put it this way: *"For we preach not ourselves, but Christ Jesus the Lord; and ourselves your servants for Jesus' sake"* (2 Corinthians 4:5). It is well known that the missionary's message must always reflect Jesus Christ. However, it is equally important that Jesus Christ *"must increase"* as the missionary's name, wishes, abilities, and accomplishments *"decrease"* as he or she serves others *"for Jesus' sake."* The missionary's service to others for Jesus Christ does not begin when he or she arrives on the field of service, but it includes those with whom he or she comes in contact while being an *"ambassador"* for Christ every day of his or her life, even while in his or her homeland (2 Corinthians 5:20).

With these biblical foundations established, the next few pages and subjects can be a spiritual encouragement and reminder of a missionary's ministry roles while on deputation and of how he or she can use this time to minister to others and bring glory to the Lord long before he or she arrives on the field of service.

Ministry or Misery

Deputation can be viewed in two ways: as God's ordained will and my extraordinary privilege to minister to those with whom I come in contact on my way to my physical destination in this world, or as a necessary evil which my family and I will endure in order to get to my goal of ministering in another place; therefore, individuals and ministries in my path are simply stepping stones to move me forward. Seeing it stated in this way, it is very easy to verbally choose the God-centered and servant-hearted philosophy. But the choices and actions that the missionary displays will be the real test of his or her view of God and his or her attitude while in His service. The Apostle Paul said, *"But godliness with contentment is great gain"* (I Timothy 6:6). Each missionary must seek to be content with God's will for both his or her present location (homeland/foreign field) and ministry (deputation/mission work) like the Apostle Paul did when he said, *"For I have learned, in whatsoever state I am, therewith to be content. I know both how to be abased, and I know how to abound: every where and in all things I am instructed both to be full and to be hungry, both to abound and to suffer need"* (Philippians 4:11–12). If a missionary does not maintain a God-centered ministry focus, he or she will find the deputation trail to be miserable. However, if that individual does maintain a God-centered ministry focus, he or she will find true security and satisfaction as he or she glorifies God with both the process and the product of his or her ministry.

The question can then be asked: What biblical truths can be applied to prevent the missionary from being miserable? **First, ministry is serving God. Ministry is not a specific location, but rather it is a heavenly vocation.** Second Corinthians 5:20 is clear that each believer is an *"ambassador"* for Jesus Christ. Therefore, each believer is representing Jesus Christ wherever he or she is located and with whomever God permits him or her to have contact.

Luke 17:7–10 says, *"But which of you, having a servant plowing or feeding cattle, will say unto him by and by, when he is come from the field, Go and sit down to meat? And will not rather say unto him, Make ready wherewith I may sup, and gird thyself, and serve me, till I have eaten and drunken; and afterward thou shalt eat and drink? Doth he thank that servant because he did the things that were commanded him? I trow not. So likewise ye, when ye shall have done all those things which are commanded you, say, We are unprofitable servants: we have done that which was our duty to do."* A true servant is faithful to his or her master, no matter where that individual is located. It does not matter if he or she is on the field or at home; that servant is always faithful to the master's wishes.

When deputation is viewed as God's place of ministry at this time, the hunger to reach the souls around the world will not be quenched, but great peace will be experienced. This is true because the missionary is in the center of God's will by obediently serving Him (Genesis 24:27). Consider this: **Will you find satisfaction by being in your country of service and out of God's will or by ministering to the souls presently around you and being in the center of God's will? Second, ministry is serving people.** Paul said, *"And I will very gladly spend and be spent for you; though the more abundantly I love you, the less I be loved"* (2 Corinthians 12:15). Paul was not concerned about the response of the people he was serving. He simply dedicated everything he was and had to serve them.

As spiritual leaders, we are admonished by the Apostle Peter to *"Feed the flock of God which is among you, taking the oversight thereof, not by constraint, but willingly..."* (1

Peter 5:2). God has clearly placed each pastor, missionary, etc. into the local church for His specific purpose.

Ephesians 4:11–12 provides the purpose of spiritual leadership when it says, *"And he gave some, apostles; and some, prophets; and some, evangelists; and some, pastors and teachers; For the perfecting of the saints, for the work of the ministry, for the edifying of the body of Christ."* This passage is part of the job description of every missionary. When he or she is on the mission field, the missionary is often a pastor, helping the flock grow in the Lord. When he is at "home," the missionary is similar to a modern-day evangelist, traveling to assist the local church leadership in teaching the flock how to grow in their knowledge of and service to their Lord.

The Apostle Paul is an example of this type of minister as he made his way to his sending church in Antioch. The Bible says, *"And when they had preached the gospel to that city, and had taught many, they returned again to Lystra, and to Iconium, and Antioch, confirming the souls of the disciples, and exhorting them to continue in the faith…they commended them to the Lord, on whom they believed"* (Acts 14:21–23). In Acts 20:32–38, he took extra time to teach and pray with those believers he was passing by. They were not seen as a means to an end but as a God-given ministry opportunity while en route to a future destination.

As a missionary on deputation, I had no idea if I was making any difference in the world. It wasn't until I was scheduling furlough meetings years later—while speaking to a supporting pastor whom I had not yet met due to a pastoral change while I was on the field—that I learned that he believed the Lord used me and the counsel I had given to direct the church to call him to be their pastor. I truly do not understand all of the reasons why God asked me to stay home a few months longer from the field, but I do know that it provided me with the opportunity to be with this ministry and have this originally unknown impact. As I look back on this and other deputation experiences, I can see that God specifically ordained all those we met along the way. I praise Him for His guidance and take hope for future travels.

Third, ministry is impacting souls, and all souls are equally important in God's eyes. A missionary trying to get to the field will naturally have his or her heart and attention drawn to his or her future home and ministry. However, it is important to remember that the instruction to *"be witnesses unto me both in Jerusalem, and in all Judaea, and in Samaria, and unto the uttermost part of the earth"* (Acts 1:8) is not only instruction to go to the uttermost parts of the world, but it is also instruction to go to your hometown and surrounding areas.

As Jesus Christ prophesied of the apostles' future ministry, He declared, *"Come ye after me, and I will make you to become fishers of men"* (Mark 1:17). Men with spiritual needs can be found even as close as next door. Although it is "religiously romantic" to write home from a faraway country about a soul saved, *"I say unto you, that likewise joy shall be in heaven over one sinner [from America] that repenteth…"* (Luke 15:7). God's desire is for all, including those at home, to hear the Gospel. In the same way, it may be "religiously romantic" to speak of believers around the world dedicating their hearts and lives to God, but God also desires this for American believers.

Each missionary should desire that God would use him or her and his or her ministry to see each believer *"draw near with a true heart in full assurance of faith, having our* [their] *hearts sprinkled from an evil conscience, and our* [their] *bodies washed with pure water. Let us* [them] *hold fast the profession of our faith without wavering; (for he is faithful that promised;) And let us* [them] *consider one another to provoke unto love and to good works: Not forsaking the assembling of ourselves* [themselves] *together, as the manner of some is; but exhorting one another: and so much the more, as ye see the day approaching"* (Hebrews 10:22–25).

A missionary must remember that the missionary with the greatest impact for the cause of Christ, the Apostle Paul, was greatly burdened for his own countrymen and said, *"I say the truth in Christ, I lie not, my conscience also bearing me witness in the Holy Ghost, That I have great heaviness and continual sorrow in my heart. For I could wish that myself were accursed from Christ for my brethren, my kinsmen according to the flesh"* (Romans 9:1–3). He boldly declared that his ministry focus was to the Gentiles and called himself *"the apostle to the Gentiles"* (Romans 11:13). But he maintained a passion for his own people and took every opportunity possible to evangelize and minister to them.

And so must the missionary fulfill his or her God-given calling to minister to those around the world while never losing his or her natural love and concern for those in his or her own country. The missionary must consider every opportunity God provides him or her to minister to his or her *"kinsmen according to the flesh"* as a privileged opportunity (Romans 9:3). This individual must say with the Apostle Paul, *"Brethren, my heart's desire and prayer to God for Israel* [my country] *is, that they might be saved"* (Romans 10:1).

As a traveling servant in the service of his Savior, it should be understood *"that the way of man is not in himself: it is not in man that walketh to direct his steps"* (Jeremiah 10:23; Psalm 37:23). God is the One planning each encounter so that the missionary has the privilege of impacting individual souls throughout all of his or her life and ministry.

As Philip was ministering in his specific revival ministry in Samaria (Acts 8:5–25), the Lord called him to a different ministry, which changed the life of the Ethiopian eunuch (Acts 8:26–29). A missionary should be equally ready to obediently go wherever, whenever, and to whomever God sends him or her.

As I returned from the field for my first furlough, my heart was greatly burdened for my homeland. I began to ask the Lord to help me be used by Him to spiritually impact the lives of those with whom I came in contact. At the end of one of our missions conferences, being thoroughly exhausted and simply looking for an opportunity to crash, I had no idea that God was going to answer my prayers. As I was loading my car with my missionary paraphernalia, a young man met me to ask some questions. My first thoughts were of how little I really wanted to talk at that time and of how little energy I had to pay attention. But the Holy Spirit quickly reminded me of my prayer to be used of God to impact others.

Little did I know that, with just a few questions about missions, God would help me to recognize that I had been praying for this young man's salvation for several weeks after having gotten to know his brother. By the end of the conversation, in the middle of the church parking lot, that young man bowed his head, and with his own words, asked Jesus Christ to forgive him of his sin and to be his personal Savior. As I walked away from that conversation, I choked back tears of joy. My strength was fully spent, and yet through the power of God, He used me to see another child added to His family.

I was quickly reminded that God wants all souls to receive His gift of eternal life, and it is His business to call me home from my "field of service" so that one of my own countrymen would be added to the kingdom of heaven. Praise God!

Be a Servant and Don't Get Used to Being Served

Jesus Christ was very clear, both by example and spoken word, about the need for believers to be servants when He said, *"If I then, your Lord and Master, have washed your feet; ye also ought to wash one another's feet. For I have given you an example, that ye should do as I have done to you"* (John 13:14–15).

There are two key lessons that need to be applied to those who travel in Christian service. **First, seek to serve others in any way possible.** God has provided each missionary with different abilities: from singing to plumbing or from children's ministry to computer knowledge. Whatever that individual's abilities are, God wishes him or her to use them to edify fellow believers and ministries (1 Corinthians 12:1–31).

A well-founded statement my parents taught me as a young person states: "Try to leave the place and people better than when you arrived." The rule of travel should be to look for opportunities to serve beyond the pulpit presentation. Look and listen for ways in which you can ease the burdens of life and ministry of those placed in your path.

In case you would argue that you have no special skills, I would suggest that washing feet does not take talent! A careful and humble look at the lives of others is all that is needed. Often this type of care will cost time and even money, but our Lord said, *"For whosoever shall give you a cup of water to drink in my name, because ye belong to Christ, verily I say unto you, he shall not lose his reward"* (Mark 9:41).

As a personal testimony, my wife and I now remember one specific church from our deputation trail—not for the love offering, meal, etc., but because of the joy we had extending ourselves to a host pastor by completing a construction project in his home. What a blessing it was to give to others while so many were giving to us!

Second, do not get used to being served. It is easy to become accustomed to special meals, words of honor, and gifts. **The idea that missionaries *deserve* this type of treatment is incorrect. They are simply recipients of the service and sacrifice of others for God (Hebrews 13:2).** Therefore, they must always remain grateful rather than expectant.

Jesus Christ could have enjoyed the luxuries of heaven (which He deserved), *"But made himself of no reputation, and took upon him the form of a servant, and was made in the likeness of men: And being found in fashion as a man, he humbled himself, and became obedient unto death, even the death of the cross"* (Philippians 2:7–8).

Luke 17:9–10 is clear" *"Doth he thank that servant because he did the things that were commanded him? I trow not. So likewise ye, when ye shall have done all those things which are commanded you, say, We are unprofitable servants: we have done that which was our duty to do."* A servant should not expect a break. That person should recognize that he or she must attend to his or her Master's wishes at all times. For this reason, this individual is ready to serve even when his or her energy is spent after a long day. The deputation trail is full of long days and frequent exhaustion, but a faithful missionary will rely on the Master's wisdom and strength to complete each ministry opportunity.

One way to test your level of servant-heartedness is to take notice of how quickly you feel slighted when you are forgotten or called upon to go above and beyond. Remember, a true servant is not hurt when he or she is treated like a servant, and that person should be humbly grateful when he or she is treated any other way (Luke 17:6–10).

Each of us, as followers of our Lord, should be willing and ready to humbly serve those around us. Jesus Christ did not only submit to the service of God the Father, but in submitting to God the Father, He also submitted to the service of men (John 13:4–17; Philippians 2:7–8). In 2 Corinthians 4:5, the Apostle Paul puts it this way: ***"For we preach not ourselves, but Christ Jesus the Lord; and ourselves your servants for Jesus' sake."***

I remember the Lord emphasizing this point in my life and ministry when I was at a pastors' fellowship. I had been in the church a few years earlier to present my ministry and had been reintroduced to the pastor that morning. That evening, as he was extending a gift to all the pastors and assistant pastors, he specifically said that he did not think that any missionaries were with them. (I was sitting only a few rows from the pulpit, and he still did not notice.) On that day, I was put to the servant's test.

Initiative or Impatience

Missionaries are known to be "go-getters." It is often this type of personality trait that God uses to bring a man or woman to the point of "laying all on the line" by serving Him around the world. Equally, the urgency of the truth, *"if our gospel be hid, it is hid to them that are lost"* (2 Corinthians 4:3), drives a missionary to love souls. The missionary desires that not one more soul from his or her field of service die and go to hell before he or she has been able to take the Gospel to them. **These two driving factors—dedication and a passion for souls—are very important in ministry, but they cannot overshadow God's will.** A missionary must be sure not to mix ministry initiative to get to the field with impatience with God's timing. He or she must *"Delight [himself] also in the LORD; and he shall give thee the desires of thine heart. Commit [his] way unto the LORD; trust also in him; and he shall bring it to pass"* (Psalms 37:4-5).

The Apostle Paul expressed his human urgency and desire to minister to the church at Rome when he said, *"For I long to see you, that I may impart unto you some spiritual gift, to the end ye may be established; That is, that I may be comforted together with you by the mutual faith both of you and me. Now I would not have you ignorant, brethren, that oftentimes I purposed to come unto you, (but was let hitherto,) that I might have some fruit among you also, even as among other Gentiles"* (Romans 1:11–13). But he prefaced his personal desires in his prayers by saying that he was, *"Making request, if by any means now at length I might have a prosperous journey by the will of God to come unto you"* (Romans 1:10). And he followed the will of God as he said, *"...but was let hitherto..."* (Romans 1:13).

Because he was not permitted to go as he desired. Paul saw that there were important ministry needs he could fulfill—in the flesh. And he could have chosen to make a trip to Rome earlier in his ministry. But he sought God's will over his personal desire and human wisdom. In the end, Paul did arrive and minister in Rome, but it was over six years after he had expressed his desire to go. When he arrived, he was in the custody of a Roman soldier and under accusation from the Jewish rulers. But he was at perfect peace, because he was in the center of God's will. **God used His means to accomplish His purpose in His timing, and in the end, He fulfilled Paul's desire.**

It is very important that a missionary rely on God's timing for the provisions needed to get him or her to the field of service with God's Gospel. The process of deputation will often test a missionary's patience, but through the process of waiting on God at home, he or she will be better prepared to be patient when the ministry calls for it on the field. The real question is: **"Do I trust God to do what is best for me and those in my field of service?"** When the answer is yes, there is a true trust in God's sovereignty, and impatience will not have the victory. Truly, James 4:13–15 must be a missionary's focus of life and ministry: *"Go to now, ye that say, To day or to morrow we will go into such a city, and continue there a year, and buy and sell, and get gain: Whereas ye know not what shall be on the morrow. For what is your life? It is even a vapour, that appeareth for a little time, and then vanisheth away. For that ye ought to say, If the Lord will, we shall live, and do this, or that."*

Patience or Complacency

A missionary must be cautious about his or her zeal and impatience. **However, it is equally important for him or her to guard against complacency while patiently awaiting God's timing.** In the early stages of deputation, the difficulties and work of constant travel and communication with pastors is new and can be difficult. But as the months and years of organization help make the deputation process a normal way of life, a missionary can find himself or herself in a new comfort zone. The future change from this newfound norm can become daunting as he or she prepares to move to another country, learn a new language, and adjust to a new culture. Although the missionary has been talking about the sacrifices ahead, he or she now realizes more fully that his or her dreams are becoming reality, and that reality is going to require another step out of that individual's comfort zone. Due to the unknown aspects of the future, a missionary, although desiring to serve God, can easily become comfortable in the present norm and, thereby, become complacent.

The children of Israel faced a similar situation. They knew that bondage in Egypt was not God's will for them any longer, and it was not what they desired either. But as they looked at the impossibilities of the Red Sea and the unknowns of the wilderness beyond (as well as fearfully looking at the physical circumstances around them), they turned to Moses and said, *"Because there were no graves in Egypt, hast thou taken us away to die in the wilderness? wherefore hast thou dealt thus with us, to carry us forth out of Egypt? Is not this the word that we did tell thee in Egypt, saying, Let us alone, that we may serve the Egyptians? For it had been better for us to serve the Egyptians, than that we should die in the wilderness"* (Exodus 14:11–12).

The Israelites lost sight of Who was guiding them to their next stage of life. Because they lacked faith in the God Who was rescuing them from bondage, they were controlled by the fear of present impossibilities and future unknowns. They decided that contentment in bondage was better than trusting God. Moses's response to the Israelites' concerns directly addressed their needs. He said, *"Fear ye not, stand still, and see the salvation of the LORD, which he will shew to you to day: for the Egyptians whom ye have seen to day, ye shall see them again no more for ever. The LORD shall fight for you, and ye shall hold your peace"* (Exodus 14:13–14). **The children of Israel needed to stop fearing the physical world. They needed to be assured that God would protect and provide for them so that they would experience** *peace.*

A missionary coming to the end of his or her deputation ministry must seriously consider the future. That individual must take time to prepare himself or herself and his or her family both physically and spiritually for the changes they will face. However, he or she should not be overcome by the unknown and thereby be content to stay in the constant mobility and instability of the traveling ministry of deputation. **He or she must look to the future through the eyes of faith and step out of his or her comfort zone, while depending on God for the security he or she will need when facing the unknown.**

Pastoral Relationships and Respect

Each missionary who is sent out by a local church has the privilege of having his or her pastor as a source of encouragement and counsel. Although each sending pastor has different talents, resources, and personalities, each one should be seen as God's source of spiritual direction throughout all of the missionary's ministry, including deputation. Ephesians 4:11 says, ***"And he gave some, apostles; and some, prophets; and some, evangelists; and some, pastors and teachers; For the perfecting of the saints, for the work of the ministry, for the edifying of the body of Christ."*** The God-given reason for church leadership is to teach and facilitate ministry participants.

What could be a better representation of this process than a missionary and his or her sending pastor? The pastor's and church's desire to be a missionary's sending church represents the relationship they have had—and desire to have—in the ministry of the missionary. Therefore, the missionary should seek to cultivate the closest relationship possible with his or her sending pastor. The missionary should seek his counsel, prayer support, and accountability (Proverbs 11:14). The missionary must recognize that he or she must do his or her part in cultivating this type of relationship. Often, during deputation, the sending pastor does not know where exactly the missionary's travels are taking him or her, or in what difficult situation he or she is finding himself or herself, but the missionary can easily share a copy of his or her calendar and be humble enough to call the pastor for counsel and prayer when he or she finds himself or herself in difficulty. The missionary can also communicate to his or her pastor the victories of the ministry, through spiritual fruit produced by the preaching or teaching of God's Word, as well as the physical fruit of financial support being supplied.

Personally, I cannot say enough about the encouragement I have received from my sending pastor. The relationship we have has been a great blessing. Because of our relationship before deputation and then the accountability that I had with him during deputation, I knew that he was always there for me and my family when I was in great need while on the field. His constant source of godly counsel and prayer support has helped us keep our focus on our Lord during some very trying times. I praise God for our relationship in ministry. I have been deeply saddened when missionaries have shared with me their sense of loss because they do not have the same relationship with their sending pastor.

As a missionary contacts other pastors, he or she must remember that they are busy. They have many pressures on their time and ministry energy. A missionary can be an extra strain on the pastor if he or she is not thoughtful in his or her communication and scheduling. For this reason, the missionary should seek to be extremely courteous at all times. If the pastor is in the middle of studying, counseling, etc., the missionary should kindly ask if he or she might call back at a better time or ask the pastor to call him or her back at his convenience. When the missionary is waiting for a call back, he or she should give ample time (days rather than hours) for the pastor to return the call.

Because every pastor has a different personality, each conversation should be handled on an individual basis. The missionary should be alert to when he or she can be a little more casual or when he or she needs to be more professional in communication. In any situation, there should be a high level of respect for each pastor, who is the Lord's servant (1 Timothy 5:1). During the early part of the conversation, the missionary should take note to the needs of the pastor (i.e., a word of encouragement) and his ministry (i.e., realistic limitations in expanding their church's missions program) by being a good and interested listener.

As scheduling becomes part of the conversation, remember that when the Apostle Paul was able, he clearly communicated his plans and intentions before his arrival (2 Corinthians 8:1–24). This should also be true of missionaries today. A missionary should know his or her schedule and where he or she might be able to be a little more flexible with the calendar in order to accommodate the pastor's ministry. However, the missionary must always be realistic with the distances that need to be traveled as well as his or her family needs, so that the visit can be a true blessing for all involved.

The decision for scheduling must always be left up to the pastor. The missionary should never be pushy or aggressive. When a pastor hesitates to schedule a meeting strictly due to financial limitations, it is best for the missionary to kindly offer to schedule the meeting and view their time together as a spiritual investment that the Lord can bless, both spiritually and physically, as He wishes.

As the meeting date arrives, the missionary must maintain a servant's heart. His or her time with the pastor and his people should be friendly, and when asked questions, informative. The missionary should look for ways to share a word of encouragement as well as a helping hand. When in the pulpit, he should remember that he is a guest in another man's ministry. A missionary's goal should be to help the pastor, as the Lord directs him, to guide and edify his flock to do the work of the ministry (Ephesians 4:11–16). When the missionary is asked questions or provides information or counsel to a church member, he or she should consider wisely his or her need to let the pastor know of the situation when necessary.

As the meeting comes to an end, the missionary must not expect more than what was previously discussed. If no financial obligations were prearranged, the missionary should not expect any. When love gifts and even support are supplied, they should be viewed as a blessing from the Lord.

Pastors are human. Therefore, the missionary may find himself or herself disappointed by the failures of some. That should never affect the missionary's attitude and respect for the God-given position each man of God holds as he leads God's people in that particular local church. A missionary should always treat elder pastors **"*as a father; and the younger men* [pastors] *as brethren*"** (1 Timothy 5:1).

Supernatural Provision or a Sales Pitch

Ultimately, if it were not for the necessity of financial support, most missionaries would never find themselves on the deputation trail. It is very easy to look at financial gain as the entire purpose for deputation, thereby, pushing the missionary into performance-based ministry, which is full of sales pitches. But Scripture is very clear that finances are not to be a believer's focus (1 Timothy 6:6–11). How, then, can a missionary make sure he or she is not a salesperson, constantly adapting and advertising his or her ministry, so that the missionary can meet his or her bottom line? How can he or she see deputation as a ministry with God's provision in mind?

First, each missionary must seek God's help to be a wise steward in his or her planning. Jesus Christ, in Luke 14:25–33, while emphasizing the need to count the cost of discipleship, used the example of an unwise man who started a building project without accurately calculating the cost. In the end, the man failed to complete the task and was mocked by those around him. The same can happen to those missionaries who have not prayerfully set an appropriate and educated budget nor sought God's timing for His full provision (James 1:5–7).

In some situations, a missionary who leaves for the field lacking support is seen as a person of great faith. However, in many cases, he or she is a person displaying his or her lack of faith. This individual has neglected to, by faith, patiently see God provide. He or she has taken matters into his or her own hands, like the children of Israel with King Saul (1 Samuel 8:5–22; 10:17–19). If he or she has asked God for wisdom in the planning, the missionary must not be "double minded" by doubting that God had guided correctly (James 1:5–8). He or she must also believe that God will supply the amount that was planned. Romans 5:3–5 tells us" ***"And not only so, but we glory in tribulations also: knowing that tribulation worketh patience; And patience, experience; and experience, hope: And hope maketh not ashamed; because the love of God is shed abroad in our hearts by the Holy Ghost which is given unto us."*** In missionary phraseology: "The trial of waiting for support produces the opportunity to gain more experience in how to trust God for future ministry, so that when I am in my country of service, I will have the hope (faith) needed to trust God's love, no matter what circumstances come my way."

Second, each missionary must look to God and not man for His supernatural provision. Jeremiah 17:5–8 says, ***"Thus saith the LORD; Cursed be the man that trusteth in man, and maketh flesh his arm, and whose heart departeth from the LORD. For he shall be like the heath in the desert, and shall not see when good cometh; but shall inhabit the parched places in the wilderness, in a salt land and not inhabited. Blessed is the man that trusteth in the LORD, and whose hope the LORD is. For he shall be as a tree planted by the waters, and that spreadeth out her roots by the river, and shall not see when heat cometh, but her leaf shall be green; and shall not be careful in the year of drought, neither shall cease from yielding fruit."* A true conviction as to Who is the true Supplier of the budget will help eliminate performance-oriented deputation ministry.** It will help the missionary feel free to serve God with all of his or her heart and ability, without the concern of gaining man's favor. Though how we represent Christ to others is always important, it is the judgment of Christ that truly counts (Matthew 10:28; 1 Corinthians 4:3–4).

In the process of serving God in the way God has directed, God will receive the glory whether support is provided or denied. Therefore, the question should not be whether or not the church will provide support but whether or not it is "God's will" for that particular ministry to be added to the ministry team at that time. By eliminating man and performance-based deputation, there is a freedom to pray to God, Who knows your needs, to be the Supplier of your needs: *"For your Father knoweth what things ye have need of, before ye ask him"* (Matthew 6:8).

A God-centered support focus will also eliminate any possible tension produced between missionaries. As each missionary understands that he or she is not competing for a prize but serving as a co-laborer in God's ministry, he or she can help others to properly glorify God and edify fellow believers. As a result, he or she will be encouraged when other missionaries receive support. And when support is personally received, the missionary will sincerely say, *"Every good gift and every perfect gift is from above, and cometh down from the Father of lights, with whom is no variableness, neither shadow of turning"* (James 1:17).

I have been asked, on several occasions about my concern for our budget needs. I am thankful to say that God has taught me that my job is to be diligent in scheduling meetings and to be a servant in each church, but it is His job to provide for my finances. For example, during our time in language school, some legitimate and unexpected changes were made to our budget. For this reason, we were placed back on the deputation trail for several months before leaving for the field. I sought God's will in our meeting schedule, and we hit the road. We spent a good number of consecutive weeks away from our home base with our three-year-old and newborn. The family struggled with sickness and exhaustion, and even more, many of the churches we visited were great ministry disappointments. At the end of this particular trip, we had only one small church added to our support list. I was reminded regularly during that time of this deputation philosophy and attempted to trust God for the outcome.

In God's own way, and to His glory, our budget was met in full, almost entirely by churches or individuals with whom we had contact previous to our language schooling. I do not know all that God wanted to do in the lives I encountered during those last months on the road, but I do know that He was putting an exclamation point on my need to trust Him with His business of getting us to the field with the budget we needed—in His timing.

Beggars Can't Be Choosers, or Can They?

Each person in ministry must take his or her responsibility to God for where he or she aligns himself in ministry affiliation, including through his or her financial support. People argue that the Gospel is the most important thing in missions. However, this is not true in any ministry, country, or culture. King Solomon said, *"Let us hear the conclusion of the whole matter: Fear God, and keep his commandments: for this is the whole duty of man. For God shall bring every work into judgment, with every secret thing, whether it be good, or whether it be evil"* (Ecclesiastes 12:13–14). Therefore, it is very important that as a missionary goes about serving God, he or she does not violate God's holiness in the process (2 Timothy 2:20–21).

Paul, while expressing the need for the Gospel to go forth, said in his second epistle to the Corinthians, *"But if our gospel be hid, it is hid to them that are lost"* (2 Corinthians 4:3). Paul was burdened with the realization that if he and fellow believers did not accomplish the ministry tasks God had given them, the lost would perish for all eternity. For this reason, he says plainly, *"Therefore seeing we have this ministry, as we have received mercy, we faint not"* (2 Corinthians 4:1).

Paul was determined to get the Gospel to the world. And he expresses his dedication to God's holiness and separation from the world in the process: *"But have renounced the hidden things of dishonesty, not walking in craftiness, nor handling the word of God deceitfully; but by manifestation of the truth commending ourselves to every man's conscience in the sight of God"* (2 Corinthians 4:2). Paul was establishing not only his battle cry for the Gospel but also for purity in presenting the Gospel. He was not only concerned with the simple message of salvation; he also rejected any form of worldly philosophy in the presentation of the message (dishonesty, craftiness, deceit), because Paul desired to be pleasing *"in the sight of God"* as he accomplished His ministry without the world's means.

In 2 Thessalonians 3:6–9 it is clear: *"Now we command you, brethren, in the name of our Lord Jesus Christ, that ye withdraw yourselves from every brother that walketh disorderly, and not after the tradition which he received of us. For yourselves know how ye ought to follow us: for we behaved not ourselves disorderly among you...."* Each missionary must be prepared to apply this command to financial support as well as to ministry participation. We must share the Gospel with the world, but we must share it based on God's holiness, with dependence on His provision and not on the world's methodology and philosophy.

Paul, while speaking about physical sustenance in 1 Corinthians 10:27–29 says, *"If any of them that believe not bid you to a feast, and ye be disposed to go; whatsoever is set before you, eat, asking no question for conscience sake. But if any man say unto you, This is offered in sacrifice unto idols, eat not for his sake that shewed it, and for conscience sake: for the earth is the Lord's, and the fulness thereof: Conscience, I say, not thine own, but of the other: for why is my liberty judged of another man's conscience?"* In Paul's teaching about eating meat, he presents a helpful biblical principle for each believer and ministry: Paul states that eating meat is fine, but if the believer knows that the meat was directly connected to an ungodly source (specifically a non-God-honoring religious practice), the meat should be rejected, based on association and testimony. For missionaries, the implication is that "beggars (missionaries) should be choosers (choosing wisely from whom they will accept support)." Each missionary must personally and prayerfully consider and apply this principle to every ministry with which he or she is associated through financial support.

I am very thankful for having learned this lesson very early in my deputation ministry. Although the experience was unpleasant, it was very protective for the future. Because of an incident that took place with one of my first scheduled churches—a situation in which I needed to take a gracious but firm stand—I became very cautious regarding the churches I was scheduling as well as those from which I would accept support. On several occasions, I experienced the rebuke of pastors as they frustratingly stated that I had no right to take such a stand and "would one day regret my decision." However, because deputation is not only about money but primarily about my fearing and honoring God, I was able to take comfort in the fact that God rewards those who seek to please Him (Psalm 58:11). As I now consider the churches that support me, I can take my furlough with joy and tranquility of heart, because we are truly on the "same page."

Being Real and Not "Just Right"

A "real" person sees himself or herself for who he or she really is before God and others. This person does not wish to over magnify his or her good traits and is honest about his or her sin. Additionally, this person recognizes the clear teaching of 1 Corinthians 4:7, as the Apostle Paul asks, *"For who maketh thee to differ from another? and what hast thou that thou didst not receive? now if thou didst receive it, why dost thou glory, as if thou hadst not received it?"* **In missions, there has been a belief—perhaps not taught directly, but caught indirectly—that missionaries are "super Christians." This is the furthest thing from the truth.** As a traveling servant of God, a missionary should be genuine with those he or she encounters by not putting on a false front.

Consider with me that **reality without a biblical perspective leads to carnality, and biblical perspective without reality leads to false piety. However, reality governed by a biblical perspective will produce true Christianity.** With this in mind, it is important that a missionary present himself or herself as a real human being who is constantly attempting to apply biblical teaching to every area of his or her life rather than one who lives above the normal events of life. The Apostle Paul was not afraid to work with his hands (Acts 18:1–3) or to share his difficulties of ministry, but he accomplished both of these with a biblical perspective (2 Corinthians 1:8–11). While sharing the realities of life, the Apostle Paul was able to communicate that, by living according to God's Word, a believer can live in this world, yet not of this world (John 17:13–21).

He also helped those reading to understand the answer to their difficulties. The answer Paul found was an eternal view of life, as he said, *"Therefore seeing we have this ministry, as we have received mercy, we faint not; But have renounced the hidden things of dishonesty, not walking in craftiness, nor handling the word of God deceitfully; but by manifestation of the truth commending ourselves to every man's conscience in the sight of God...but though our outward man perish, yet the inward man is renewed day by day. For our light affliction, which is but for a moment, worketh for us a far more exceeding and eternal weight of glory; While we look not at the things which are seen, but at the things which are not seen: for the things which are seen are temporal; but the things which are not seen are eternal"* (2 Corinthians 4:1–2, 16–18). This is the same answer that needs to be presented today. It is very easy to act "just right" for a few hours in a host home or church. **But if acting "just right" is actually covering up truth or conforming for a moment, there is danger of presenting a lie.** If, when we are shown to be what we truly are—an average human sinner saved by the grace of God and now seeking to serve Him faithfully—we respond biblically, we will have a great opportunity to share with others the answers they need for their lives as well.

Please understand, this does not give permission for sinful habits. Romans 6:1–2 is very clear as it says, *"What shall we say then? Shall we continue in sin, that grace may abound? God forbid. How shall we, that are dead to sin, live any longer therein?"* The Apostle Paul was revealing his personal struggles with sin in Romans 7. While he revealed his private battle with sin for all to see, he also provided the solution of focusing on Christ when he said, *"For the law of the Spirit of life in Christ Jesus hath made me free from the law of sin and death"* (Romans 8:2).

On several occasions, my wife and I have been complimented for being "real people." I am not always sure what an individual is saying when he or she says that we are "real" in comparison to others who are not. Perhaps that person is speaking about my inabilities, and he or she can identify with them. I do not know. But I am reminded that Romans 12:3 says, *"For I say, through the grace given unto me, to every man that is among you, not to think of himself more highly than he ought to think; but to think soberly, according as God hath dealt to every man the measure of faith."*

I clearly recognize the need to not "hang out the dirty laundry," but there should be a willingness to acknowledge that missionaries also put on their shirts one sleeve at a time. Missionaries are real people with real needs (personal, marital, parental, etc.) and must make God real in every area of their lives and ministries.

It is also very helpful for a missionary to show that he or she can be a part of everyday life tasks. The missionary must demonstrate a willingness to get dirty fixing a car or taking out the garbage. The Bible says, *"Whether therefore ye eat, or drink, or whatsoever ye do, do all to the glory of God"* (1 Corinthians 10:31). Based on this command, each missionary should look for the opportunity to teach and exemplify to fellow believers that this command is universal. All believers, including missionaries, have the same ability and responsibility to glorify God, while at home completing daily tasks or around the world preaching the Gospel.

As I look at my life, I cannot find any way to cover up that I am an ordinary guy. I identify easily with 1 Corinthians 1:25–31, which says, *"Because the foolishness of God is wiser than men; and the weakness of God is stronger than men. For ye see your calling, brethren, how that not many wise men after the flesh, not many mighty, not many noble, are called: But God hath chosen the foolish things of the world to confound the wise; and God hath chosen the weak things of the world to confound the things which are mighty; And base things of the world, and things which are despised, hath God chosen, yea, and things which are not, to bring to nought things that are: That no flesh should glory in his presence. But of him are ye in Christ Jesus, who of God is made unto us wisdom, and righteousness, and sanctification, and redemption: That, according as it is written, He that glorieth, let him glory in the Lord."*

Each missionary should be able to say with the Apostle Paul, *"And I thank Christ Jesus our Lord, who hath enabled me, for that he counted me faithful, putting me into the ministry"* (1 Timothy 1:12). This individual should recognize that his or her ministry position does not set him or her apart from others. He or she can greatly aid fellow believers by being honest about how he or she seeks to live a God-centered life, even in the menial tasks of life.

From a Glass House to a Glass Suitcase

On many occasions, the home of a family in ministry is described as being a "glass house." This term represents the teaching found in James 3:1–3, which says, *"My brethren, be not many masters, knowing that we shall receive the greater condemnation. For in many things we offend all...."* James immediately applies his teaching to the tongue, but the idea that there is more *"condemnation"* for a leader and that he or she is constantly in the position to *"offend"* can be applied to every area of life. Often church members, fellow pastors, and even the lost are watching every aspect of the minister's life and family, including what goes on in the home.

For a missionary, his or her home is a suitcase. Although it is unpleasant and intrusive to have your luggage searched at the airport, it can be even more unpleasant to have fellow pastors, believers, and even the lost looking through your private life on a regular basis. For many individuals, a suitcase represents vacation. For a missionary, it represents getting to work and the need to be on guard. He or she, and each member of his or her family, will be watched very closely until they once again return to their home (if they have a home base at all). Although a missionary's life is similar to a pastor's life (living in a glass house), he or she has an added set of unknowns that demand an even greater amount of care. A pastor, over time, has the ability to know the expectations of his ministry, people, and town, but a missionary does not have the same privilege. From week to week, he or she is with different ministries, pastors, and believers who all have their own expectations based on their individual ideas. **Even more difficult for the missionary is that he or she must carry his glass suitcase into the ministries and homes of these evaluating eyes, to be placed on display.**

Now that we have seen the difficult truth of a deputation missionary's life in this figurative fashion, what focus should he or she maintain in order not to become overwhelmed by the watchfulness of others or from embarrassment and shame from what others find in his or her suitcase?

First, accept that the watchfulness of others is taught in Scripture. As already mentioned, James 3:1–3 is very clear about the responsibility of each leader. The qualifications of a pastor (which include a missionary) provide other believers with the responsibility of evaluating the minister's home (within reason) to make sure that he fits the standards God places on him (1 Timothy 3:1–7; Titus 1:6–9). **A missionary attempting to fulfill God's qualifications will not fear the eyes of others but will see them as God's means of accountability in his or her life.** He or she will find that the accountability of others can be a great blessing in providing proper protection from failing and becoming disqualified.

Second, accept that God's judgment is more important than man's. Paul said, *"But with me it is a very small thing that I should be judged of you, or of man's judgment…but he that judgeth me is the Lord"* (1 Corinthians 4:3–4). Each family, whether in church leadership or not, should seek to follow biblical teaching on the family (Ephesians 5:22–6:4). When this teaching is practiced, there will be little for others to condemn. Because God's Word is being followed, the family can anticipate God's approval and blessing.

Third, accept the burden of giving up your rights so that God and His Word can be magnified in the lives of others. Paul expressed his willingness to sacrifice for the sake of ministry, as he said, *"For though I be free from all men, yet have I made myself servant unto all, that I might gain the more…. And this I do for the gospel's sake, that I might be partaker thereof with you"* (I Corinthians 9:19-23). Paul also said, *"Have we not power to eat and to drink? Have we not power to lead about a sister, a wife, as well as other apostles, and as the brethren of the Lord, and Cephas? Or I only and Barnabas, have not we power to forbear working?... Nevertheless we have not used this power; but suffer all things, lest we should hinder the gospel of Christ"* (1 Corinthians 9:4-12). He was interested in using his liberty, not *"for an occasion to the flesh, but by love serve[ing] one another"* (Galatians 5:13).

It might be expressed in this way: "God can use you to serve others only as much as you are willing to sacrifice your self-service." Each ministry family should be willing to take the "high road" in order to broaden their ministry impact (1 Corinthians 8:13).

Fourth, accept that not everyone can be pleased. Romans 12:18 states, *"If it be possible, as much as lieth in you, live peaceably with all men."* The command of God is that each believer seek to be in harmony with other believers. An important note is that the responsibility is based on the qualification of: *"as much as lieth in you."*

There are times when there is a lack of knowledge or there are difficult circumstances in which an offence is unavoidable. On other occasions, the expectations of others are unreasonable due to a lack of understanding or kindness on their part. In either case, the missionary should provide apologies where necessary and should see the situation as an opportunity of learning for the future.

The Apostle Paul received the criticisms of others whom he had been seeking to serve. His response was simple: he shared the facts of the matter and expressed his desire to not have his ministry limited in the lives of those to whom he was ministering (1 Corinthians 9:1–12).

Fifth, accept the need to pull down the shades. Just as there is a time and place to close the shades of a home to provide privacy and rest, there is a need to shield the traveling family from the constant pressure of the ministry. Jesus Christ sought refuge from the crowds for Himself and His disciples by going into the mountains (Matthew 14:23; Mark 6:31). For a traveling ministry family, it may require a few days away from the spotlight by staying at home or by finding a private place for vacation. A missionary must not feel limited by his or her spouse and family but rather recognize that God acknowledges his or her limitations in ministry in order to care for them. First Corinthians 7:32-33 says, *"But I would have you without carefulness. He that is unmarried careth for the things that belong to the Lord, how he may please the Lord: But he that is married careth for the things that are of the world, how he may please his wife."* A person's need to take time for his or her family is not condemned by God but rather taught by God. And during this time of rest, he or she must follow Jesus' example of growing closer to God the Father through the spiritual refreshment of prayer during times of rest and refuge (Luke 5:14).

As I look back on our travels, an incident of being on display comes to mind. We arrived in the town of the church in just enough time to stop at a fast-food restaurant for dinner, just before the evening service. We ate our meal, minded our own business, and made our way to the church. That evening, a church member told me that he was at the same restaurant where we had been. He watched our family conduct themselves during dinner and concluded that it was quite possible that we were the missionaries in town. That evening, he was pleased to find not just our ministry in the service to be an encouragement to him but our dinner as well.

On another occasion, as I pulled into a gas station, a good distance from any ministries to which we were connected, my wife cautioned me about making sure that I did not park in a parking place designated for those who are handicapped. She especially noted that there was a police officer parked just a few places to the side of us. I parked our vehicle in the parking place alongside the handicapped location and entered the gas station to get what I needed. As I paid for my food, the officer approached me and began to question me about my field of service (I had not mentioned to anyone there that I was a missionary). He then asked if my last name was Markle. With what I'm sure was a nervous tone, I answered, "Yes."

He then gave me the break I needed. He had not looked up my license plate, nor was my picture posted on the "most wanted" ads! He had been at one of our supporting churches just a few weeks earlier (even though it was a good distance away) when we had presented our ministry update. Thankfully, he shared with me that our ministry and presentation had been a blessing to him, and I was on my way with only a questioning look on my wife's face as she watched the situation from the car. With these examples, as well as many, many more, I have been reminded that friends, family, and even enemies are watching my family and me at all times. No matter what gas station, restaurant, shopping center, etc. I enter, there is a good chance that, as God expands my ministry influence, my ministry accountability is expanded as well.

***

Practical Application

As a note of practical application to these biblical observations and the responsibility of the ministry family, please permit me to make a few simple suggestions.

1. Allow the watchful eyes of others to be a source of biblical accountability and appreciate the fact that, through the

observations of others, you can be sure to maintain a biblically based family.

2. Remember that first impressions can last a lifetime. Therefore, arrive at the church or host home in attire and with actions that truly represent your heart for the Lord.

3. It is much easier to prevent your children from sharing family secrets if there aren't any! If what is talked about, listened to, watched, and participated in within the privacy of your home, car, hotel, etc. is pleasing to the Lord, what your children talk about and display an interest in will be less questionable.

4. Make sure that as you seek to minister to others, the entire family is biblically aligned one with another. When necessary, take the time to make any corrections before placing yourself under the scrutiny of others. Also, do not hesitate to excuse yourself when issues arrive during your visit, so that you can quickly make corrections.

5. Be careful about what you pack in your suitcase, car, etc. Each item seen as yours will directly reflect on your ministry, family, and your view of God (including, but not limited to: clothes, games, books, toys, music, movies, etc.).

6. Don't make excuses when you find yourself in an awkward situation because you or your children have unintentionally violated another individual's standards. Simply apologize when necessary and take steps to correct the situation. By handling the situation correctly, you may be displaying a greater testimony than if the situation had never arisen.

7. Make time for family privacy by scheduling time away from the ministry spotlight. This may involve finding a hotel away from churches in between meetings or special times at parks and museums where the family can simply be family.

8. Make time for marital privacy. Take advantage of trusted family members who offer to care for the children for a few hours while you go out alone, or ask them to take the children out to a park or to eat so you can stay home and enjoy just being alone—together.

Faithfulness or Failure

Deputation is not a downhill hike or an easy stroll on level terrain. It has its rough and uphill climbs. But the Bible is clear when it says, *"Moreover it is required in stewards, that a man be found faithful"* (1 Corinthians 4:2). **A man, woman, and family who will not trust God's will, love, provision, etc. while in their home country will find it very difficult to trust God in a foreign country, culture, and language.**

For this reason, as a missionary seeks to give his or her all to God, he or she must claim the promise that: *"My God shall supply all your [his] need according to his riches in glory by Christ Jesus"* (Philippians 4:19). He or she must say, as the Apostle Paul did, with a determined heart, *"Therefore seeing we have this ministry, as we have received mercy, we faint not"* (2 Corinthians 4:1). Paul faced trials and tribulations, but whether he was at his sending church, on a missionary journey, or in prison, he was able to say, *"I have fought a good fight, I have finished my course, I have kept the faith: Henceforth there is laid up for me a crown of righteousness, which the Lord, the righteous judge, shall give me at that day: and not to me only, but unto all them also that love his appearing"* (2 Timothy 4:7–8).

There is comfort found in Paul's words: *"That he which hath begun a good work in you will perform it until the day of Jesus Christ"* (Philippians 1:6). With this promise in mind, each missionary can be assured that the Lord has started a work in him or her that is "good," and every part of the deputation experience is part of His perfect will. Therefore, each experience is for the missionary's best, and there is no reason for failure (Romans 8:28–30; 1 Peter 1:3–8).

I will not be so unkind as to misrepresent the reality of constant travel and the burdens of the deputation ministry, but I can reassure you with a common and yet far from trite statement that: *"We know that all things work together for good to them that love God, to them who are the called according to his purpose"* (Romans 8:28). **God is working and will not fail you. He asks you to be faithful by being full of faith.**

As the work becomes hard and little fruit seems to be produced, I encourage you that: *"Though our outward man perish, yet the inward man is renewed day by day"* (2 Corinthians 4:16). Truly, God wishes you to learn the valuable lesson of His consistent love while at home so that you can recall it and depend on it when you are far, far away from home (Romans 5:3–5; 8:35–39). *". . . Brethren, be not weary in well doing"* (2 Thessalonians 3:13). But rather, *". . . Be ye stedfast, unmoveable, always abounding in the work of the Lord, forasmuch as ye know that your labour is not in vain in the Lord"* (1 Corinthians 15:58).

Preaching:
Performance or Proclamation

Each missionary has the privileged responsibility to speak in the pulpits of many churches and to impact the lives of many individuals during his deputation travels. Each of these opportunities should be taken seriously and should be dedicated to the service of the Lord. For this reason, his goal for each message should be to present an accurate view of God and each individual's responsibility to act according to a biblical fear of God in every area of his or her life (Ecclesiastes 12:13–14). The missionary's message should be applicable to each listener and should be representative of Paul's heart in Romans 12:1–2, where he states, *"I beseech you therefore, brethren, by the mercies of God, that ye present your bodies a living sacrifice, holy, acceptable unto God, which is your reasonable service. And be not conformed to this world: but be ye transformed by the renewing of your mind, that ye may prove what is that good, and acceptable, and perfect, will of God."*

The missionary should be committed to not allow any lackadaisical practices to become part of his pulpit ministry. **First, a missionary should not take for granted the opportunities he has to preach in other men's pulpits.** In many situations, the missionary has not yet earned the respect of the people nor labored to produce the crowd. He has simply shown up at the gracious invitation of the pastor. With this invitation, he has become a "hireling" shepherd for a time (John 10:12–13), but he must not abuse his privileges.

Second, a missionary should not "perform" in the pulpit but rather should clearly proclaim God's Word. The pulpit should not be used as a tool to gain the favor of the people or as a competition (especially during a missions conference). The

Apostle Paul said, *"And I, brethren, when I came to you, came not with excellency of speech or of wisdom, declaring unto you the testimony of God. For I determined not to know any thing among you, save Jesus Christ, and him crucified. And I was with you in weakness, and in fear, and in much trembling. And my speech and my preaching was not with enticing words of man's wisdom, but in demonstration of the Spirit and of power: That your faith should not stand in the wisdom of men, but in the power of God"* (1 Corinthians 2:1–5).

The missionary's responsibility is: *"As every man hath received the gift, even so minister the same one to another, as good stewards of the manifold grace of God. If any man speak, let him speak as the oracles of God; if any man minister, let him do it as of the ability which God giveth: that God in all things may be glorified through Jesus Christ, to whom be praise and dominion for ever and ever. Amen"* (1 Peter 4:10–11). While recognizing that each preacher has his own style of preaching based on the gifts God has given him, each preacher should seek to use his gifts, based on God's power, to glorify Him through the proclamation of His Word (Colossians 3:23–24).

I was deeply saddened when a pastor asked me why it was that many missionaries were not good preachers. This should not be the case. If a missionary does not have a passion to grow in his ability to clearly, accurately and convincingly communicate the Word of God in his own language, how will he ever be able to do so in a foreign language? A missionary should constantly be looking for ways to improve the clarity of his pulpit ministry, which is the proclamation of God's Word. He must follow the Apostle Paul's counsel to Timothy when he said, *"Till I come, give attendance to reading, to exhortation, to doctrine. Neglect not the gift that is in thee, which was given thee by prophecy, with the laying on of the hands of the presbytery. Meditate upon these things; give thyself wholly to them; that thy profiting may appear to all. Take heed unto thyself, and unto the doctrine; continue in them: for in doing this thou shalt both save thyself, and them that hear thee"* (1 Timothy 4:13–16).

Third, a missionary should be alert to the audience to whom he is preaching. Because the crowd is different at each church, it is very possible that God would have a different message for each crowd. He should never accept the idea that he needs only a few sermons for the deputation ministry. Although, in the end, he may use only a few key sermons, it is important that a constant study of God's Word provide a fresh look at new and old passages in order to have a proper application of those passages.

A missionary's philosophy for studying should be found in Paul's command: **"*Study to shew thyself approved unto God, a workman that needeth not to be ashamed, rightly dividing the word of truth*"** (2 Timothy 2:15). The missionary must always spend time praying and asking the Lord's direction for each message before each service. When the message text is a previously used text, the missionary must still be sensitive to the Holy Spirit's direction in the presentation of the text, because no two audiences are the same, and the Holy Spirit knows what practical applications are specifically needed for each particular audience.

Fourth, the well-known missionary passages are very powerful (Matthew 4:35; 9:35–38; 28:18–20; Acts 1:8, etc.), **but they should not be the only texts preached.** Although missions, the idea of serving God around the world, is very important and is directly connected to a missionary's presence in the pulpit, it is also very important that he consider other key subjects in his preaching. Often there is a need to step away from the common passages dealing with "going" in order to prepare the believers to be ready to go as *"vessels meet for the master's use"* (2 Timothy 2:19–21). Also, the well-known passages are often repeated by many missionaries and, thereby, become mundane and commonplace. When a missionary opens God's Word and proclaims a biblical truth that is applicable to every believer in the congregation, the Holy Spirit can then use the passage to take those particular believers He chooses to the point of making a missionary decision.

    For example:
Message of Discipleship – Luke 14:25–33
    *All believers should be willing to give all to God, and those whom God calls to be missionaries will go out of obedience to God's specific will for their lives.
Message of Dedication – 2 Corinthians 4:1–18
    *Every believer should be fulfilling his or her ministry responsibilities for God until the day God calls him or her home, and those God wishes to send around the world will need the same level of dedication.
Message of Dependence – 2 Corinthians 1:3–11
    *Each believer faces trials and needs to know that God is a comforting God. Those who serve God in foreign countries will be able to take comfort in the same biblical truths.
Message of Destination – Acts 8:26–40
    *Each believer should be ready to serve God wherever God has placed him or her, whether the location of service is at home or in another country.
Message of Distance – Philippians 1:3–11
    *Each believer knows of individuals whom they desire to see live for God, and this same desire can be applied to the missionary who is far away from his or her family and friends (while on the field) or from his or her home congregation (on furlough).
Message of Purity – Isaiah 6:1–8

> *Each believer should understand his or her unworthiness in comparison to God and should be ready to accept God's call to go anywhere for service after he or she has found God's forgiveness.
>
> Message of Prayerful Participation – Romans 15:30–33; Colossians 4:2–4; 1 Thessalonians 5:24–28; 2 Thessalonians 3:1–7; Ephesians 6:18–20; Hebrews 13:18
>
> *Each believer can participate in the ministry through prayer. It is helpful for there to be a clear knowledge of how to pray and what to pray for on behalf of those in ministry, both in the States and on the field.

These are but a few of the many passages of Scripture and biblical examples that can help each believer grow—not only in his or her understanding of missions but also in his or her personal dedication and service for the Lord.

Fifth, the area of financial need must be presented with discretion. Although there is a time and place for preaching about the subject of giving, this is an area that can be easily abused by missionaries. In the missionary's zeal to get to the field and the recognition that his budget must be met, it is easy for a missionary's preaching to become full of pleas for financial giving. Although there is a great need for giving, the focus of the preaching should be on reaching the believer's heart and not his or her wallet (2 Corinthians 8:1–5). When a believer's heart is reached, he or she will have a desire to place his or her treasure in the very same place (Matthew 6:19–21). There is no reason for a missionary to be known as a "moochinary!"

Time Spent or Time Invested

Spending is not always wrong. Money is spent on needed food, housing, clothes, etc., each of which are good choices. But when extra care and effort are taken to invest money, the rewards, although not immediately gratifying, are greatly multiplied for the future. This same truth can be applied to time. The missionary must spend time on the daily responsibilities and current ministries. This spending is correct and should be done with great dedication. However, like money, time should be wisely invested for the future. Although it may not be necessary for the missionary to have a new sermon each week (or even four per week, like when he is planting a church), he should be investing his time into the study of God's Word and working to prepare himself for his future ministry when time and resources will be greatly limited.

Paul's advice to Timothy was: *"Study to shew thyself approved unto God, a workman that needeth not to be ashamed, rightly dividing the word of truth"* (2 Timothy 2:15). **Through the study of Scripture during deputation, a young missionary can be refining his doctrinal statement, honing his ministry philosophy, and grounding himself in the faith** (Romans 10:17). Paul provided godly counsel again to Timothy when he said, *"But refuse profane and old wives' fables, and exercise thyself rather unto godliness"* (1 Timothy 4:7). And he also stated, *"Till I come, give attendance to reading, to exhortation, to doctrine. Neglect not the gift that is in thee, which was given thee by prophecy, with the laying on of the hands of the presbytery. Meditate upon these things; give thyself wholly to them; that thy profiting may appear to all. Take heed unto thyself, and unto the doctrine; continue in them: for in doing this thou shalt both save thyself, and them that hear thee"* (1 Timothy 4:13–16).

Each missionary must guard himself or herself against wasting time through worldly pleasures (Internet, social media, video games, sports, etc.) or ministry distractions (foolish hobby horses and useless arguments of the day). The Apostle Paul warned Timothy by saying, *"Flee also youthful lusts: but follow righteousness, faith, charity, peace, with them that call on the Lord out of a pure heart. But foolish and unlearned questions avoid, knowing that they do gender strifes"* (2 Timothy 2:22–23). **When a missionary focuses on fulfilling God's call for his life by knowing and practicing sound doctrine, that individual has the promise that he or she will be able to make a protective impact in the lives of those to whom he or she will minister in the future—as well as to himself or herself.**

Ephesians 5:14–16 says, *"Wherefore he saith, Awake thou that sleepest, and arise from the dead, and Christ shall give thee light. See then that ye walk circumspectly, not as fools, but as wise, Redeeming the time, because the days are evil."* How applicable for a missionary who will be living in a country and culture that is filled with evil. **Each missionary must search God's Word to know how to redeem his or her time for God's glory in every circumstance of life and ministry both in his or her homeland and on the foreign field.**

A missionary who is willing to take the answers of Scripture to the lost world must be prepared with the right answers to the world's questions. Colossians 4:5–6 explains how he or she can have wisdom to deal with all those he or she encounters, as it says, *"Walk in wisdom toward them that are without, redeeming the time. Let your speech be alway with grace, seasoned with salt, that ye may know how ye ought to answer every man."*

As an added point of admonition, **the prefield ministry, when used as a time of study, is the perfect opportunity for the missionary to glean the spiritual depth needed to get him or her through the extreme difficulties he or she and his or her family will face within the first days, months, and even years of being on the field.** The deputation trail should be viewed as a spiritual boot camp in which the soldier of the cross takes time to *"exercise"* himself or herself *"unto godliness,"* so that he or she is prepared with the spiritual strength and skills necessary to fight the battles that lie ahead (1 Timothy 4:7).

This boot camp can assure the missionary that he or she will *"continue in the faith grounded and settled, and be not moved away from the hope of the gospel, which ye have [he has] heard, and which was preached to every creature which is under heaven"* (Colossians 1:23). Each missionary must heed the command to: *"Continue thou in the things which thou hast learned and hast been assured of, knowing of whom thou hast learned them; And that from a child thou hast known the holy scriptures, which are able to make thee wise unto salvation through faith which is in Christ Jesus. All scripture is given by inspiration of God, and is profitable for doctrine, for reproof, for correction, for instruction in righteousness: That the man of God may be perfect, throughly furnished unto all good works"* (2 Timothy 3:14–17)

I am very thankful for the time I had to study and prepare for my future ministry during my years of deputation. The subjects and passages the Lord led me to study during our prefield ministry became great sources of spiritual strength and helped to guide me to build a biblically based ministry on the field.

DEPUTATION PRACTICE

The process of planning and preparing for deputation can be very overwhelming. It is as if each missionary needs to become the CEO of his or her own company. But, different from a CEO, the missionary will need to be all of the branch managers and work force—all at the same time (communication director, advertising specialist, shipping and transportation planner, etc.). The organization process takes time, and many times things are forgotten. It is because of the difficulty of this very important area of ministry that I want to share with you a few helpful tips that span many different subjects found in the deputation ministry. Please use these tips not as the final rule book, but as guides to help you formulate your own personal deputation practices.

Helpful Tips
To avoid the potholes
Along the deputation trail.

1. Contact lists
    A. Contact lists can be gathered through the home pastor, family and friends, mission board, other supporting pastors (after you have built a rapport with them), etc.
        *Be very careful of lists provided by other missionaries due to the over-taxing of pastors and their ministries.
    B. Each contact should be evaluated based on location and ministry separation issues.
        *Personal recommendations from trusted pastors and faithful believers can ensure good visits with churches of like faith and practice.
        *Each contact should be considered with care. With the resources of the Internet, etc., you should complete a proper investigation in order to protect awkward circumstances due to separation issues.
    C. The opportunity to make contacts by being a guest at a pastor's fellowship should never be abused.
        *In loving respect for pastor's, DO NOT be aggressive at pastor's fellowships, but rather enjoy the opportunity to get to know those men God allows you to meet and ask God to open their heart with interest in your ministry, family, and field of service

2. Meeting locations
   A. It is beneficial for missionaries to make contact "hubs" surrounding their home church or where they have friends or family as a central location. These contacts can work to help them schedule meetings as well as be a place of fellowship they return to for future furloughs.

      *When the original contact lists from friends, family, etc. have been exhausted and you need to expand the contact resources, maintain the hub philosophy as much as possible. It may be possible to find a location that has a prophet's chamber as a central location for a time, or, by contacting board pastors, you may find ministries of like faith and practice in a specific geographic location.

      *It may also be helpful to connect the hubs by looking for contacts between two or three hubs so that travel time on furlough can be useful as you link your supporting churches while coming and going from different hubs.

   B. Computer and Internet mapping programs can be a great help to find approximate distances from one place to the next and make boundaries as to how far you will go for a meeting.

      *For example: a part-time deputation missionary must be able to return to work on Monday, so by using a mapping program, he or she can find all of the contacts he or she has available within three hours of his or her home and not contact anyone beyond that distance to get started. This type of planning will help for scheduling furlough and prevent wasted funds on travel expenses.

Helpful Tips

    C. Although GPS units and smart phones have become very popular and are very helpful, it is always important to double check the directions the unit gives before setting out on a trip. (It is not uncommon for a GPS to take you out of your way and waste valuable time while getting you to your destination.)

    D. A missionary should plan on arriving at least thirty minutes before the first service of the day. This will allow him or her time to greet and communicate with the pastor as well as set up all of his or her display and multimedia presentation.

3. Intro packets *(Supplementary Examples)*

    A. Each missionary should prepare some form of introductory letter and portfolio (or brochure) that can be sent to each pastor.

        *You should view the portfolio's price in printing and mailing as an investment and not a loss. You can easily recover the cost of each packet when you scheduled meetings gain support.

        *The portfolio content should be brief, yet thorough, in content. The more information the pastor has about the missionary and his or her ministry, the fewer questions the missionary will need to answer and clarify over the phone.

        *The portfolio should be as professional as possible—quality printing, proofreading, layout, etc.

        *The portfolio should be reviewed by the home pastor and any others who might be able to provide clarity. Make sure that you are not just presenting information correctly but also that you are communicating your heart correctly.

*The portfolio should be distinguishable by use of a specific color of folder, design, or label on the front. This will help the pastor remember your portfolio when you contact him.

B. It is best to mail a small portfolio of information to a pastor two weeks before calling to ask for a meeting.

*If the pastor has received the packet of information, it is much easier for the missionary to explain his or her ministry and family, because most the information has already been in the pastor's hands. By mailing a packet, the missionary also shows proper respect for the limited time of the pastor, and demonstrates that he or she desires to represent the Lord's ministry in the best way possible.

*Have digital copies of the portfolio information on hand to quickly e-mail them to any pastors who may like to have computerized copies.

*Although many churches enjoy the ease of digital data from their missionaries, neither a web page nor digital communication can replace the benefits of a good first impression. A professional-looking portfolio is the best introduction. Then the pastor can easily review at his convenience and then investigate further through web- based resources such as video presentation, current prayer letter, doctrinal statement, etc., that are referenced in the portfolio.

C. The following should be inside the portfolio:
1. Prayer card
2. Personal salvation testimonies
3. Call to ministry
4. Explanation of ministry experience

5. Explanation of desired ministry in the field of service and God's leading to that ministry
6. Purpose statement(s) for the ministry that is being presented
7. Letter from the home pastor
8. Copy of a recent prayer letter
9. Prestamped, self-addressed post card (optional, but useful to save the missionary money and time for follow-up phone calls).
10. Ministry DVD – It may be possible to include a DVD of a multimedia presentation and/or digital copies of your packet information.

*Although DVDs are helpful, they can also be a hindrance. Not every DVD will work in every machine, and not every pastor will have knowledge or time to look at the entire presentation. A digital presentation can be helpful, but it cannot replace printed documentation.

D. Have a well-written doctrinal statement available to send to any pastor at his request.

4. Communication

*Clear and respectful communication always helps to make each ministry opportunity move more smoothly. Proper communication during deputation is very important: it represents the missionary's dedication to and forms of communication for the future, when there is a great distance between the pastor and missionary, and accountability will only be limited to written form.

A. Introduction Packet - By sending out informative packets to pastors in advance, the missionary shows his or her understanding of the pastor's time

restraint and his or her desire to be transparent about his or her life and ministry.
B. Phone Calls - By keeping phone calls friendly and yet informative, the missionary a true heart for people and ministries.
   *Out of kindness for the pastor, his staff, and family, there should be ample time given for returned phone calls (2 days) and a limited number (3) of messages should be left if no reply is received. Also, no phone calls should be made to the pastor's home or cell phone unless permission is specifically given.
   *All messages left on voice-mail or with a secretary should be short yet informative: name, mission agency, field of service, description of the portfolio, contact phone number.
   *The missionary should be ready to share a brief description of his family, ministry, and availability while being ready to answer any questions the pastor may have.
   *The missionary must be diligent to get basic information about his participation in the ministry when a meeting is scheduled: dates, times of services, ministry involvement, hospitality, etc.
C. Confirmation Letters - By sending confirmation letters, the missionary shows attention to organization and details. *(Supplementary Examples)*
   *The missionary should express gratitude for the interest expressed in his family and ministry as well as confirm the dates and details of the scheduled meeting.
D. Confirmation Phone Calls - By making a confirmation phone call two weeks prior to the

meeting date, the missionary is able to verify and clarify all of the final details for hospitality and his ministry involvement: arrival and departure times, service times, ministry opportunities, meals, housing, etc.

*The missionary should always be flexible to adjust previously made plans for the pastor's and ministry's current needs, and he should never impose himself on the pastor or people for accommodations or hospitality (allow the pastor to set the schedule and offer hospitality arrangements).

E. E-mail Communication - By using e-mail communication when possible, the missionary displays his or her understanding of quick and concise communication. The missionary must realize that e-mail is very impersonal. It may also be important to make sure the message was received by the right person.

*Each e-mail should include a "read receipt" so that there is no question that the note was received.

*It may be necessary to follow up e-mail communication with a final phone call in order to make sure that there is verbal confirmation of all the details.

F. By presenting regular (at least once quarterly) prayer letters, the missionary communicates his or her understanding of accountability and willingness to share his or her life and ministry with those who are assisting that missionary for years to come.

G. By sending a year-end ministry letter directly to the pastors of the churches that have expressed continued interest, the missionary will be able to

keep himself or herself accountable and the pastor informed as to the progress of the ministry on a yearly basis.
- H. By sending timely and personal thank-you notes, the missionary will show a heart of gratitude.
  - *Each church the missionary visits should receive a thank-you note (within two weeks) for the time given to present the ministry, for the love gift, and for any personal blessings received.
  - *Each host family should receive a thank-you note for their personal service to the Lord by opening their home (the thank-you note can be left at the home as the missionary leaves).
  - *Each family providing a meal should receive a thank-you note for their kindness and generosity (it may be important to get the home address from the pastor, or if no address is available, send the note to the church to be given to the family).

5. Prayer letters
   - A. Send a prayer letter out in a timely manner and on a regular basis (every two or three months).
     - *Using e-mail can help save some money.
     - *Local churches should always receive a physical copy so that it can be posted publically.
     - *Blogging and overwriting (writing too frequently) can become a burden on the time of the missionary and receivers. If a missionary is going to start this style of communication, he or she must be sure that he or she can continue it.
   - B. A prayer letter should be as professional and attractive as possible.
   - C. The prayer letter's letterhead should include:

Helpful Tips

        1. Family picture
        2. Contact addresses for the missionary, the home church, and the mission board
        3. A symbol or picture representing the field of service (flag, map, etc.)
    D. The prayer letter should not be shallow in content. It should discreetly provide information about the present situation in ministry, family news, prayer requests, and praises of how God has answered previous prayer requests.
        *A prayer letter may present needs, but it should never be a "want ad."
        *A prayer letter may be honest about difficulties, but it should never be used as an opportunity to complain.
    E. The prayer letter should be seen as a "praise" letter as well. It is important to communicate to the "prayers" as God answers their prayers.
    F. The prayer letter should be written in such a way that a summary of prayer requests and praises can be made very quickly.
        *This may include an actual listing or bolding of the key points and requests.

6. Calendar
    A. A missionary must be carefully accurate and detailed in his or her scheduling.
    B. Meetings should not be a great distance from each other.
    C. A missionary should try to be with the church all day if possible so he or she can truly get to know the church and so that the churches can get to know the missionary.
        *The missionary must be as flexible as possible and prepared to be involved in any aspect of the

ministry: children's ministry, teen ministry, senior's ministry, banquets, conferences, work days, etc.
- D. A missionary must also take into consideration the needs of his or her family while he or she schedules each meeting and conference.
  *Because the qualifications of a pastor/missionary include the family—and the family will all be ministering together—it is very important that the family travels with the missionary at all times unless there is sickness or extreme circumstances.
- E. A missionary must remember that many pastors are scheduled at least six months in advance.
  *When it is possible to fill dates closer to the call date, do so, but the missionary should not expect more than is reasonably possible from the pastor.

7. Records
  *Proper record keeping is of the utmost importance. The ability to recall messages preached, hosts' names, etc. can be very helpful. With today's technology, a missionary can find a database that will help him or her with many of these details.
  - A. A database should be established which can keep track of records for every visit. For example:
    *Microsoft Outlook can be used for basic information, but it is not very helpful for many ministry details.
    *"Act" by Sage is a user-friendly database source, but it does have some limitations.
    *Google resources can be helpful as it will communicate with computers, tablets, and smart phones.

Helpful Tips

        1. Contact information
        2. Meeting dates
        3. Messages preached
        4. Host families
        5. Support and love offering amounts
   B. Written copies of church information should be printable for easy references and travel purposes.
   C. All digital files should be backed up regularly!
   D. An organized and printable (distributable) list of all prayer letter contacts, which includes both mailing and e-mail addresses, can be a great help in the prayer letter process.

8. Display
   *Be prepared to intelligently answer questions about any display items.
   A. For practical purposes, the display and table knick-knacks should be easily portable as well as sturdy.
      *Be prepared for tables of all sizes. Although it is good to have a large display board for viewing purposes, it may be impractical when a church can only provide a small table.
      *Because of the amount of transportation, it may be wise to use a sturdy suitcase with wheels to easily and safely pack and transport all of the supplies.
   B. The display board should clearly present:
        1. Family (name, picture, etc.)
        2. Field of service (a map, flag, and some simple facts)
        3. Purpose of serving (church planting, teaching, etc.)
        4. People who are going to be reached (represented in picture form)

*Digital picture frames have been well received and have, in many ways, replaced the photo album.

C. All printing done for the display board should be large enough for any individual to read; it should also be concise enough to not take up too much time in reading.
    *It is always helpful to have theme colors and bright, attractive backgrounds and printing formats.
D. The table of knick-knacks should include little representations of the culture and people of the country.
    *It is always helpful to provide the opportunity for children to touch and even play with a few objects.
E. It is important to provide plenty of prayer cards in a neat display.
F. When permitted by the pastor, use a small sign-up sheet for prayer letters (a 3x5 card flip chart works well) to gather prayer support for the future.
G. As a point of ministry presentation, when possible, present a Bible, tracts, etc. in the language of service with an English copy alongside so that interested individuals can see and compare the language difference.
    *Be mindful that with the material you choose to place on your display, you will be making a statement regarding your doctrinal position and affiliation.
    *Be mindful that people will take things from your display, not realizing that they are not for distribution. For this reason, when possible,

Helpful Tips

have extra copies of any materials you are displaying.

9. Prayer card
   A. Prayer cards should always be as professional and as durable as possible (including at least one side in full color).
   B. Prayer cards of both large (4x6 or bookmark) and small sizes (business-card size) can be a great help to those who have different ways of remembering and praying for missionaries.
   C. Prayer card pictures and information should truly represent the country of service and the type of ministry to be accomplished.
   D. Prayer cards should include:
      1. Family name
      2. Name of each family member (ages and birthdays are helpful as well)
      3. Recent photo of the family (Sunday dress attire for all during deputation)
      4. Theme verse
      5. Pictures of nationals
      6. Pictures from the country of service: landscape, flag, map, etc.
         *Double check the pictures and any graphics to make sure they are fully accurate.
      7. Contact information: missionary, home church, mission board
         a. Phone numbers
         b. Mailing address
         c. E-mail address and other internet addresses

10. Multimedia presentation
    A. The presentation should be eight to twelve minutes long.
    B. The presentation should be fully narrated and include appropriate musical background (the music you choose will speak directly to your personal separation position).
        *Personal touches can be added by using several different family members as part of the narration, but this should only be done when professionalism is not in jeopardy.
        *Obtain the necessary permission to use the music so that copyright laws are not violated.
    C. Although limitations may occur, each picture should be either taken by or include the missionary so that there is no misrepresentation of the picture and the message it is being used to convey.
    D. The presentation should clearly present:
        (The more information provided, the fewer questions will be asked or need clarification during question-and-answer times.)
        1. An introduction of the missionary family
        2. The Lord's leading in personal testimony and in preparation for future ministry
        3. The field of service (some small details about the country, culture, language, religion, etc.)
        4. The people who will be the focus of the ministry
        5. A few brief ways in which the help of the believers watching can be involved in this particular ministry as well as other ministries (prayer, physical help, etc.)
            *It is also very good to provide a challenge for the believers to be serving

God in their present ministry as well as wherever God might lead them in the future.
- E. Have all of the needed equipment on hand to accomplish the presentation (with the exception of a screen).
  1. Projector
  2. Computer/DVD players
  3. Adaptor cables for sound
  4. Extension cord
  5. Small speakers
- F. The presentation should be in an easily adaptable format(s) so that the church that has its own equipment can quickly make the presentation without many difficulties.

  *If a church has its own projector, etc., it is always best to use their equipment, because it has been purchased for their sound and lighting conditions, and the people are accustomed to the quality of the equipment.

11. Questions and answers

    *Over time, the missionary will find that certain questions are standard, and for these questions, he or she can formulate a well-rounded answer that has been refined over time (sometimes these answers come with greater explanation than the question originally is asking for, but with the explanation, many other questions are put to silence).
    - A. Pastoral questions

      *A missionary should be prepared to provide pastors with biblically-based answers to the following:
      1. Doctrinal questions
      2. Bible version questions

3. Family and ministry philosophy questions
   *Including dress, music, and video standards
4. Personal and public ministry separation questions
5. Personal spiritual walk and witnessing opportunities in the present
6. Mission board information and other ministry affiliations

B. Public questions

*The missionary should welcome public questions. The opportunity for churches to ask questions publicly always places the missionary at a disadvantage. Although a missionary should know about his or her field of service, there may be questions where you may need to provide the "I don't know" answer. Be humble enough to say, "I don't know," and yet interested enough to offer to look for the answer if there is a real need to do so.

1. Family questions
   a. What will you do for schooling for your children?
   b. What is the role of your wife in family and ministry?
   c. Where will you live in relation to your ministry?
   d. What safety and health issues will you face?
   e. What are your budgeting needs—dollar amount and percent?
      *It is important to be able to provide a brief breakdown of your budgeting needs (possibly including some economic

information) to show how much of the budget is for ministry, personal, taxes, insurance, etc.
   f. What plans are there to include the children in language learning?
2. Ministry questions
   a. How did God lead you to your field of service?
   b. What type of ministry will you be involved in: church, school, etc.?
   c. Where will you be serving: city, country, etc.?
   d. Will you have coworkers?
   e. How will you accomplish evangelism and discipleship?
   f. Will you need language training, and where will it be?
   g. Would it be possible to have mission trip groups in the future?
   h. What are some long-term and short-term goals?
   i. What other fundamental works and missionaries are in the area?
   j. What are some of the key hindrances you will face?
3. Country questions
   a. Where is your country?
   b. What is the size and population of the country?
   c. What type of foods do the people eat?
   d. What is the economic condition of the country, including cost of living?

  e. What is the political situation, and how will it affect you as a missionary?
   *Including the view of the US and Americans
  f. What are the primary religions?
  g. What is the primary language?
  h. Are the people receptive or resistant to the Gospel?
C. Private questions
  *Many private questions will be the same as the pastoral and public questions. However, it may be necessary to provide a little more background information or details in order to be a little more personal.
  *Some private questions may seem intrusive. Unfortunately, not every question is presented with tact or is thought about before being asked. In these situations, do not show any signs of shock, but rather relay an appropriate answer in a tactful manner.
  *Some private questions should be answered with care. Because of a missionary's direct connection to the spiritual authority of the pulpit ministry, a missionary must be very careful in his or her answers to any doctrinal or controversial current subject. In many cases, direct, brief answers from a passage of Scripture can be helpful, but there must always be an alertness to the fact that the question may be asked because the individual asking has a difference of opinion with the church leadership. It is very important that missionaries quickly refer individuals back to their local church for any detailed answers and in-depth

counsel. The "loaded" questions can sometimes become the questions that blow up in the missionary's face and destroy ministries.

12. Proclamation of Biblical Truths
    A. The message should be a highlight of the missionary's ministry to the church.
       *Through the message chosen and the presentation of that message, the church will have the opportunity to see the missionary's commitment to God and His Word, as well as his passion for others.
    B. The message must always be found to be doctrinally and contextually sound.
    C. The message should be appropriate for the audience, service time, and the stated objectives of the pastor.
    D. The message should presented with clarity and authority.

13. Meal time
    A. Meals are a great way to get to know other believers in a more casual setting. However, it is not uncommon for the missionary to never really get to finish his or her food. While others are eating, the missionary is often answering questions and sharing more about the ministry.
       *When possible, try not to dominate the conversation, but rather give the listener the opportunity to share his or her life and ministry as well.
    B. Meal time is also a great way for the hosts to see you interact as a family. Whether it is easy or not, the entire family is on display in what and how they eat. This can be a great opportunity for the

missionary to show his or her biblical understanding of taking care of his or her family even while under ministry pressures by simply asking to be excused from a conversation so that he or she can help with the children, etc. Although some will not understand this need, many will, and they will take note of the proper role of parenting being balanced with the opportunities for ministry.

C. In many homes, it is necessary to eat what is provided. If for some reason this is impossible, a request to be excused from this unwritten rule may be in order. Because each meal is different and the missionary is at the mercy of the host, the missionary should not feel overly pressured but should follow common courtesy (Luke 10:8). For those with specific health needs or small children, it is always beneficial to mention needs before arriving.

*Although very difficult, it may be necessary to allow the children to have more sweets, drinks, etc. than normally desired. Though this may be intruding into family habits, it is often best to accept the kindness of the hosts rather than to offend them by refusing what they have graciously provided.

D. When at a restaurant, it is important that the missionary be moderate in his or her purchase. On some occasions, the family providing the meal would not normally eat at a restaurant, but it is a treat for them, just as it is for the missionary.

*When reasonably possible, ask for any leftovers to be taken with you in an effort to not waste the gifts others have given to you.

Helpful Tips

14. Overnight stays
    A. Staying in the home of a church member or pastor can be a great way to get to know the ministry better. However, great caution must be used. It is always best for the entire family to stay together in the same home so that no problems arise with the children without parental protection or discipline.
    B. Although all accommodations are not like home, the missionary should view each host family as sacrificing a great deal of themselves to have an extra family in their home during this time. Be flexible and defer to the host in areas of meal times, bathroom needs, bed times, etc. In many cases, these issues will not be a problem; however, if there is a conflict, attempt to adjust yourself and your family, because the host has already sacrificed to have you with them.
    C. It is very important to recognize that not every pastor knows what goes on in the homes of his church members. On occasion, you will find questionable materials in kids' rooms, music selections, etc. If this occurs and you feel the need to share it with the pastor, please do so discreetly and with Christian love. Also, be aware that a home is not the full representation of the ministry, and do not take a bad circumstance as a direct reflection of the pastor's ministry.
    D. You are never to "make yourself at home," even when told to do so. Each person understands that his or her home runs differently and has certain standards and norms. Because you may not know the norms of the home where you are staying, accept the statement "make yourself at home," as a kind gesture, but still be alert and respectful to

what permissions they truly mean by that statement.
- E. Double check scheduling for the host family (work, school, etc.) to avoid the chance that two individuals of the opposite sex would be left in the home alone at any given time.
- F. When overnight accommodations are not suggested or provided by the church, it may be best, out of kindness, to not ask. Although it may be an oversight on the part of the pastor, it may also be that they do not have the ability to provide the needed accommodations. In this situation, view your time and expense as part of your ministry and look to the Lord for His provision.

*If no housing accommodations are mentioned, you may need to look for hotel accommodations close to the church. However, it may be wise to find accommodations outside of the church's town to prevent any awkward moments.

15. Packing

*Each family and ministry will have specific needs as they pack. For this reason, it may be helpful (at least in the beginning) to set up check sheets for each family member, so that nothing is left behind.

*As you arrive in town, it may be helpful to note where Walmart, Kmart, and pharmacies are located, so that if there are any items left behind, you can acquire them quickly and discreetly. Here are some packing ideas and suggestions:

- A. Roof racks are helpful, but tail racks and boxes are much handier. No matter what cargo containers you use, they must be fully secure at all times.

Helpful Tips

B. Vehicle repair tools (spare tire, jack, jumper cables, wrenches, etc.) should always be in the vehicle.
C. Small first-aid kit with bandages, pain killers, children's medicine, etc. should be easily accessible.
D. Small cooler of snacks and drinks may be handy for long trips.
  *It may be helpful to have a small snack and drink in your suitcase in case you a need to eat something small between meals or before bed.
E. Bedding for the children (sleeping bags, pillows, etc.)
Pillows for the parents (you don't need to take these in, but have them available for naps in the car and for any lack at the host home).

SUPPLEMENTARY EXAMPLES

Personal Testimonies

Supplementary Examples

Jeremy Markle

My personal testimony begins before the time of my birth. My parents had surrendered their lives to the Lord. They promised Him that they would attempt to raise up children who would be saved at a young age and who would learn to love Him as they grew into adulthood. Based on this commitment, my father, while holding me for the first time on the day of my birth, shared with me the simple plan of salvation. Although I cannot remember this occasion, my parents' fervent prayers, faithful example, and continual Gospel witness led me to understand my need of Jesus Christ as Savior at the age of three.

I recall jumping into my parents' bed and asking my mother how I could know that I was on my way to heaven. She immediately referred me to my father, who explained the Gospel in its entirety to me. Although I do not remember every verse that he showed me or every word that I said, I know that I bowed my head, and in simple, childlike faith, I accepted Christ as my personal Savior (John 3:16; Mark 10:14–15).

Romans 10:11 says that, "Whosoever believeth on him shall not be ashamed." God immediately gave me a desire to see my best friend accept Jesus Christ as Savior. That desire was enhanced after my family moved, and I, at the age of five, wrote him a letter and placed a tract in it, praying that he would read it and get saved. Two weeks following my salvation, I obeyed the Lord in believer's baptism.

I am assured that I am a child of God, because as I look back at my life, I can see His conviction and work. If I could not see God's chastising hand, I could not claim to be one of His children (Heb. 12:6–8).

Laura Markle

 I was eight years old when my church, Fairview Baptist Church of Great Falls, Montana, was having evangelistic meetings with Evangelist Ken Lynch. I was not paying attention during the service. I do not remember what Mr. Lynch preached. However, at the time of the invitation, I knew, when he asked if anyone had not accepted Christ, that I had not done so, and that I needed to do so. I realized that I was a sinner doomed for hell, and that only the blood of Jesus Christ could save me. I went forward and accepted Christ as my Savior. I was baptized three years later when I was eleven years old.

John 6:44
"No man can come to me, except the Father which hath sent me draw him: and I will raise him up at the last day."

Supplementary Examples

The Markles' Purpose

Jeremy and Laura Markle have purposed in their hearts to follow God's Word and the Holy Spirit's leading in their lives and ministry. Their ministry's purpose is based on God's commission to all believers. Matthew 28:19–20:

18 And Jesus came and spake unto them, saying, All power is given unto me in heaven and in earth.

19 Go ye therefore, and teach all nations, baptizing them in the name of the Father, and of the Son, and of the Holy Ghost:

20 Teaching them to observe all things whatsoever I have commanded you: and, lo, I am with you alway, even unto the end of the world. Amen.

We purpose to follow God's commission based on Jesus Christ's authority over all things, including our lives. It is Christ Who is King of kings and Lord of lords, and we wish to keep Him on the throne of our hearts (Romans 12:1–2).

We purpose to be God's ambassadors to a lost world in which we live by sharing the Gospel of Jesus Christ (2 Corinthians 5:20–21).

We purpose to go forth with the truth of the Scripture to teach believers to identify with their Savior through the waters of baptism by immersion. We recognize the importance of this first step of obedience (Acts 2:41–42).

We purpose to disciple and edify each believer through the Word of God. We believe that the local church is God's source of fellowship and spiritual edification for all believers (Hebrews 10:24–25).

We purpose to live our lives according to the truth that Jesus Christ is always with us. We will accept this truth as a source of accountability in the decisions we make and as a source of comfort during life's circumstances (Hebrews 13:15).

Supplementary Examples

Jeremy's Call to Ministry

I believe that any man's call to ministry is located within God's perfect will for his entire life (Rom. 12:1–2). Today, God does not stop men on the road as He did with Saul (Paul), nor does He speak in a small voice as He did to Samuel (1 Sam. 3:1–15; Acts 9:1–9). However, I believe that a present-day calling to the ministry is just as substantial. Today, God uses the Holy Spirit to guide His children through His Word into a willing obedience of His will (John 16:13). I believe that the Apostle Paul, although called by an audible voice, followed the leading of the Holy Spirit to fulfill his calling (Acts 18:21; Rom 1:10; 15:32; 1 Cor. 4:19). The Holy Spirit is also the One Who places an unquenchable desire in a man for the purpose of being a minister of the Gospel of Peace (Psa. 37:3–5; 1 Tim. 3:1). I have submitted myself to the request that God makes for ambassadors (Isa. 6:13; Rom. 10:13–15).

My call to the ministry began when I was a small boy. After I accepted Jesus Christ as my personal Savior, He began to work on my heart about lost souls. During this time, I had the privilege of watching my father work as a minister of God. Moving into my teenage years, God was continually attempting to make a strong-willed child into a moldable young man. During my junior and senior years of high school, God led my father and our family into the Water of Life Ministry based out of Airport Road Baptist Church, Allentown, Pennsylvania. My father believed that he was not the only one who should be involved in this ministry, but that his entire family should be a part of God's work.

At this time, God permitted me to go on a ten-day missions trip to Puerto Rico. God used this trip and the other ministries in which I was involved—both with my father and at Airport Road Baptist Church—to impress on me a strong burden for the lost and for the pastoral ministry. God also used the lukewarm teens in my Christian school and youth group, along with the opportunity to minister to other teens while traveling with my father, to teach me the difference between living for the world and living for God (Matt. 6:24). My desire was deepened for dying to this world and for living unto Christ and Christ alone (Gal. 2:20).

Following my years in high school, I followed the Lord's leading to Northland Baptist Bible College, where I majored in youth ministries. During all four years at NBBC, God opened the door for me to work in extension churches where I was able to put my training into action. This training also furthered my desire for full-time Christian service. After graduation, God allowed me to work for a short time in Marshfield, Wisconsin, as a full-time assistant pastor. I continued to find God's call into the ministry stamped more deeply on my heart. God then chose to move me to work in Melvin, Michigan, with my brother, who is the pastor of Melvin Baptist Church. During this time, I was unable to be paid full-time, so I also worked a secular job. Working in the secular work world gave me a great opportunity to share the Gospel, and once again, God drove the desire for full-time Christian service deeper.

God's will for each individual is private and personal. However, I believe that others can see God's leading in an individual's life. I also believe that good, godly advice is essential in finding God's will (1 Kings 1:6–7; Pro. 11:14). Through the ministries with which I have come in contact, I have been warned of the difficulties and encouraged by the joys of the ministry, but I have never been discouraged from my calling.

Those who are called into the ministry must be able to fulfill the requirements for ministers as set down in Scripture. These requirements are found in 2 Tim. 3:1–9 and Titus 1:5–9. I believe that I can fulfill these requirements. This is not to say

Supplementary Examples

that I do not have areas in which I need to grow, but I believe that God has preserved my life to be able to be used for Him according to these requirements for the ministry.

In a man's call for ministry, his wife and family must also be considered. My wife has surrendered her life to full-time ministry through God's special guiding hand. God has allowed her to see the hardships in ministry, yet she has been and is willing to follow His leading. Ultimately, she believes her first calling is to be my wife, and in that calling she is committed to follow me wherever I believe God is leading us (Ruth 1:16–18; Eph. 5:22–25). Our desire for our children is that God would permit us to raise up the next generation of believers who will serve Him with their whole hearts (Josh 24:15; Pro. 22:6; Eph. 6:4).

In looking for God's perfect will for my life, I have sought for His guidance in several areas. First, I surrendered my life to full-time service, if that would be His will. In answer, He has placed an unending desire for the ministry in my heart (1 Sam. 3; Rom. 12:1–2; 1 Tim. 3:1). Second, I have seen God's guidance, preservation, and preparation of my life for ministry (Jud. 6:36–40; Ps. 37:3–5; Pro. 3:5–12; 2 Tim 3:14–4:5). Third, I have spent much time in prayer seeking God's direction and have found His answer to be a continual, "Yes" (Gen. 24:12–14, 25:26–27; Ps. 32:8–9; James 1:5). Finally, I have sought advice and godly counsel from pastors, family, and friends and have found them all to be encouraging me into the ministry (1 Kings 1:6–7; Pro. 11:14). Based on these steps in my life, I believe it is God's will for me to be a minister of the Gospel of peace. God has given me the great responsibility to "preach the word; be instant in season, out of season; reprove, rebuke, exhort with all longsuffering and doctrine" (2 Tim. 4:2). (Gen. 24–25; Judg. 6–8:3; 1 Sam. 23:1–5)

Supplementary Examples

God's Leading to Puerto Rico

Jeremy Markle

During my junior and senior years of high school, God's guiding hand began to prepare my heart for serving Him in Puerto Rico. During these two years, God began to direct my heart through His Word and the Holy Spirit's conviction that I must be willing to surrender all of my life to Him. He also permitted me the privilege of participating in a ten-day missions trip to Puerto Rico with a sister church to my home church, Airport Road Baptist Church of Allentown, Pennsylvania. This trip focused on a one-week Vacation Bible School. During the next year, God continued to direct my heart toward the Puerto Rican people through serving in the bus ministry and living in an inner-city environment that was heavily populated by Puerto Ricans.

At the close of my high school years, the Lord guided me to further my education at Northland Baptist Bible College. During my junior year of college, I was approached by several other students to speak to the school missions department with a request for a trip to Puerto Rico. When I approached the missions department, they encouraged me to follow through with this endeavor, and they gave me general guidelines to help. This trip was for two weeks and involved four college students besides myself (one being Laura), one high school student, and a Spanish-speaking couple. We were able to assist Paula VanNatta, a BWM single missionary, with teen-focused revival meetings. We were also able to minister to other missionaries on the island.

The Deputation Trail

In May of 1998, Laura and I graduated from Northland, I with a BA in youth ministries, and Laura received a BS in elementary education. We were married in June of 1998. God graciously led me to a position as the assistant pastor of Grace Baptist Church in Marshfield, Wisconsin. We had been serving at Grace Baptist during our senior year at Northland.

As God continued to work in my heart, my brother Scott, a pastor in Melvin, Michigan, invited me to come and assist him in his ministry. This was one of the greatest blessings I have received. It was not only an opportunity to work with family, whom I knew God was calling me to leave in the future, but it was also truly a fulfilment of a lifelong desire to work with family in ministry for at least a short time. Knowing that God had not called me to stay indefinitely with my brother, I began spending much time in prayer, seeking God's direction for a church which would be willing to consider being our sending church to Puerto Rico. During this time, I was able to have contact once again with Pastor Stoeckmann of Airport Road Baptist Church (currently known as Valleyview Baptist Church). He extended an invitation to Laura and me to come and join the ministry there and see if God would make them our sending church. This also was a display of God fulfilling one of my desires.

We made the move back to my home area of the Lehigh Valley in Pennsylvania, and we have enjoyed the opportunity to participate in the ministry of Valleyview Baptist Church. One of our highlights was when Pastor Stoeckmann asked me to organize my third trip back to Puerto Rico and to be accompanied by several church members. This trip came about in August of 2001, and it was focused on helping a missionary who was just starting a work on the southern side of the island. Laura and I stayed on the island one extra week to survey the island and to observe the ministries that currently exist.

With these few reflections on how God has led me to a ministry among the Puerto Rican people, I must say that these are only the tip of the iceberg in comparison to how He has

Supplementary Examples

guided day by day to confirm His leading. Every fork in the road and every hurdle that has been crossed has only given me a greater sense that God was doing this work in our lives.

I want to give Him the praise and glory that He deserves. I am also eagerly waiting to see how He will continue to confirm His plan for our lives

Laura Markle

When I was in eleventh grade, we had a missions conference at my church, Parsippany Baptist Church in Parsippany, New Jersey. Some national pastors from Argentina had come for the conference, and my family had them over for dinner at our house. Because I was taking Spanish classes that year, the pastors and I were chatting in Spanish. They told me that I should consider coming to Argentina as a missionary. This was the first time I had ever considered missions. Later that spring, I decided to take the opportunity of going on a missions trip to Brazil to see if the Lord would really have me go into missions. On that trip, I learned that missions is very much like ministry here in the States, and that God could use me if I would let Him. I surrendered to missions.

I attended Northland Baptist Bible College with a major in Elementary Education, with the focus of using my degree on the mission field to teach missionary children. During college, I went on a missions trip to Mexico, and the Lord reaffirmed in my heart the desire to go into missions. I was also able to go to Puerto Rico on a missions trip with Jeremy during our college years.

I am excited about going to Puerto Rico. The Lord has given me a burden for these wonderful people. While my primary focus is to be the best helpmeet for my husband and mother for my children that I can be, I do desire to serve the Puerto Rican people in any way possible

Supplementary Examples

Confirmation Letter

January 14, 2004

Dear Pastor (   ),

I would like to confirm the details of our conversation on (   ).

My wife, Laura, our son, Jeremiah, and I are looking forward to joining you for your (   ). As discussed, we are planning on ministering by (   ). We are also planning on setting up a display to present our ministry purpose and field of Puerto Rico. We would ask that you would help us by providing a table for our display and a screen and microphone cord for our slide presentation.

Please do not hesitate to communicate any other areas of service in which we may be of help to you and your congregation.

I have enclosed a short introduction of our family and ministry that can be used as a bulletin insert if you would like.

I will look forward to confirming these details approximately two weeks prior to the meeting date.

If you have any questions, concerns, or alterations, please contact me via the resources below or by calling my cell phone at (610) 360-8201.

In Christ's service,

Jeremy Markle.

Other Ministry Resources Available From Walking in the WORD Ministries

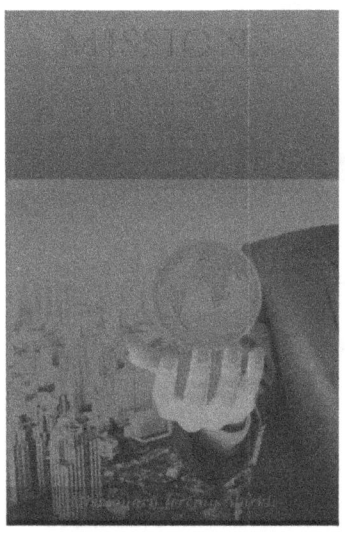

Missions: Ministering Beyond Our Borders was written to provide insight into the physical, emotional, and spiritual adjustments a missionary faces as he begins his new life and ministry. Throughout its pages you will find spiritual encouragements for the missionary and helpful hints for his family and friends who desire to support him in his service to their Lord and Savior Jesus Christ. There is also "Missionary Edition" which provides a large appendix with additional tips specifically for missionaries.

Marriage: A Covenant Before God presents 10 biblical studies about marriage, each one is based on the marital relationship of Adam and Eve and has the purpose of helping young couples understand God's plan and purpose for their life together. Included are practical questions, illustrations, and applications for each biblical truth in order that the couple might grow in their knowledge of each other and how they can glorify God together.

www.walkinginthewordministries.net

www.ingramcontent.com/pod-product-compliance
Lightning Source LLC
Chambersburg PA
CBHW071311060426
42444CB00034B/1895